# Well Played, Saffron!

by Tara Dodson
illustrated by Andy Rowland

Saffron's sister played chess. At weekends, Saffron went to chess club with her.

One day, Saffron did not want to go.

“Can I play at Dean’s house today?” asked Saffron.

"Yes!" said Dad. "We will drop you off on the way."

“Shay can come with me!” said Saffron.

She grabbed Shay’s ball and lead.

“Stay still, Shay!” said Saffron.

Dean was in his garden.

“Come and play cricket,” said Dean.

"I have never played cricket," said Saffron.
"I might not be very good."

Dean tried to teach Saffron how to play.

"It is hard but fun," said Saffron.

Dad picked Saffron up.

“I want to join a cricket team!” said Saffron.

The next week, Saffron went to cricket training. Dean helped to tie on her pads.

Saffron hit the ball a long way. She felt proud.

"You should come back next week!" said Dean.

"Yes, I love it!" said Saffron.

“We will play in this contest,” the coach said.

“Our team might win!” said Dean.

Saffron trained each day in her garden.

Saffron counted down the days. She could not wait to play in the contest.

On the day, Saffron's legs felt weak.
She wanted to play well for her team.

Soon, it was Saffron's turn to bat.

"You can do it, Saffron!" shouted Dean.

Saffron swung her bat. She missed the ball. It hit the stumps so she was out.

Saffron sat back down. She felt upset but she wanted to support her team.

Then Saffron's team had to bowl. There was one ball left. The batter hit the ball and ran.

Saffron reached out and grabbed the ball. She hurled it back to her team.

The ball hit the stumps. The batter was out. Saffron's team were the winners!

"I love throwing cricket balls," said Saffron.
"I love throwing balls for Shay, too!"

# Look Back

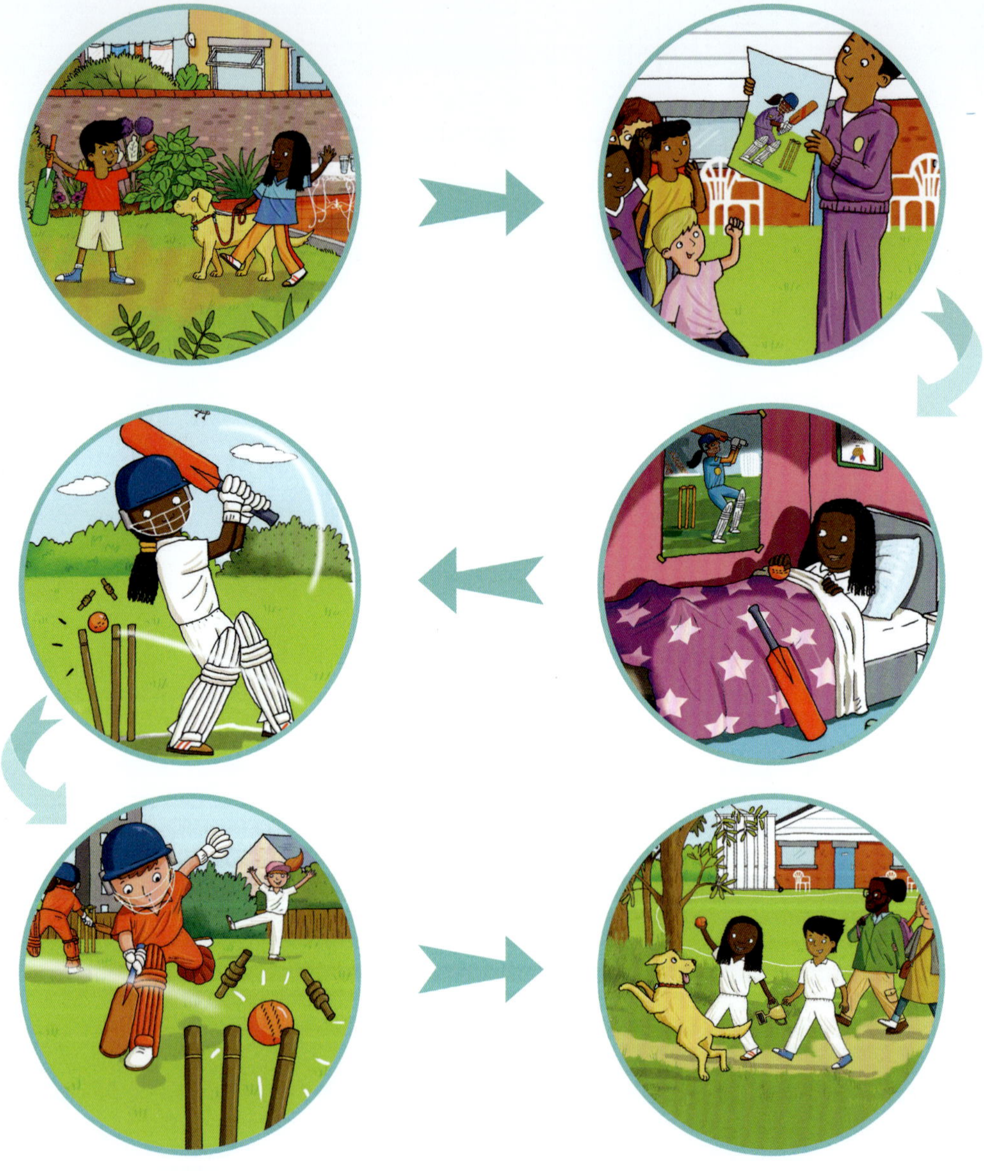

Encourage students to use the pictures to retell the story.